BRITISH MILITARY BAND
CAVALRY
REGIMENTS

WENDY SKILTON

Midland Publishing

CONTENTS

THE AUTHOR

Wendy Skilton is a Director of Music in Miniature, a military figurine company specialising in bands of the British armed forces.

She is a confirmed Royalist with a deep passion for preserving military traditions, customs and legacies and the National Heritage of Britain. She is a member of the International Military Music Society and has had several articles published on British Military Bands

Wendy is married with two daughters and lives with her husband in Leicestershire.

ACKNOWLEDGEMENTS

My thanks are due to all the Bandmasters and many Bandsmen who have helped in compiling the information, in particular my sincere thanks to WO1 David Cresswell (QRIH) whose help has been invaluable. Also I would like to express my gratitude for the use of photographs supplied by various regiments. All other photographs are from my own collection.

Wendy Skilton 1992

Illustration captions:

Front cover: *Drum Horse 'Winston', Queen's Royal Irish Hussars.*
Title page: *Drum Horse 'Dettingen', Queen's Own Hussars.*
Back cover: *Royal Scots Dragoon Guards at the Edinburgh Tatoo.*
Opposite page: *An 'impromptu' instruction in the art of conducting by the Bandmaster of the 16th/5th Queen's Royal Lancers*

First published in the UK in 1992 by
Midland Publishing Limited
24 The Hollow, Earl Shilton Leicester, LE9 7NA

ISBN 1 85780 006 0

Design by Words & Images, Speldhurst, Kent, and Midland Publishing Limited.
Printed and bound in England by
Printhaus Book Company, Northampton.

INTRODUCTION

For the past three hundred years British Cavalry regiments have been the envy of the world. Awesome in battle and spectacular in dress they have become a part of British national heritage.

With the advent of khaki, and later the camouflage dress, ceremonial uniforms were phased out along with the noble horse, who has been replaced by the tank and other armoured vehicles. Only the Household Cavalry, the King's Troop (Royal Horse Artillery) and the Guard's Division are provided with full ceremonial uniforms at public expense. The remainder of the army being given No 1 dress, temperate ceremonial uniform, usually referred to as 'blues'. However, these regiments are permitted to retain their full ceremonial uniform for use by the bands, corps of drums, pipers and trumpeters at the regiment's own expense.

Some cavalry regiments have also been granted permission to retain their drum horses, a beautiful spectacle of a 'bygone age' but one which is very popular with all those who go to see the bands perform. At the turn of the century every cavalry regiment had its own drum horse, proudly displaying their battle honours on the drum banners. Today, other than the Household Cavalry, only three regiments now have a drum horse. Each horse carries a pair of kettle drums, one being slightly larger than the other, giving a range of an octave between them, and they are struck about halfway between the centre and the edge.

It is the purpose of this book to pay tribute to the cavalry regiments of the British Army and record the ceremonial uniforms worn by the bandsmen. Originally cavalry regiments were divided into heavy, medium and light. Heavy cavalry were comprised of the Household regiments, the Scots Greys and Dragoons; medium calvary comprised of Dragoon Guards and Lancers; light cavalry was totally made up from the Hussar regiments. Thus, this book will follow along the same lines, putting each regiment in order of precedence within the cavalry: Dragoon Guards, Lancers and Hussars.

From left to right: *Director of Music, Blues & Royals; Bandmasters, Royal Scots Dragoon Guards:*
14th/20th King's Hussars and the 5th Royal Inniskilling Dragoon Guards.

DRAGOON GUARDS

Bandmaster, The Royal Scots Dragoon Guards.   RSDG

At present there are four regiments of Dragoon Guards:

The 1st The Queen's Dragoon Guards
The Royal Scots Dragoon Guards
The 4th/7th Royal Dragoon Guards
The 5th Royal Inniskilling Dragoon Guards

With the exception of the Royal Scots Dragoon Guards, whose uniforms will be dealt with under the regimental heading, the items of dress for Dragoon Guards are basically the same.

The helmet is made of polished metal with a brass cross-piece and plume holder on the top. The plume, once made of horse hair is now made of nylon with the colour varying according to the regiment. The chin-chain is also brass, backed by leather and held in place on either side of the helmet by a brass rosette. Across the front, just above the peak, there is a laurel-leaf design in brass surmounted by the helmet plate in the centre. The plate displays the regimental number which is encircled by a brass rim bearing the motto, this in turn is surrounded by a white metal twelve pointed star in the form of rays.

The tunic is made of serge material, cut square in the front with a high standing collar and shoulder straps. Collars, shoulder straps, the front edge of the tunic and the rear of the skirts are all piped, the colour varying according to the regiment. The piping around the top of the cuffs is known as the 'Austrian knot' pattern. Originally worn by Austrian troops it was adopted by the British army during the nineteenth cen-tury. All buttons are 'stay-bright', with eight on the front, eight on the rear skirt and one on each shoulder strap.

Cavalry pattern trousers have a 1¾″ stripe down each outer seam and short cavalry boots with white metal box spurs are worn.

The pouch belt, once made of leather, is now made of thick white plastic with a 'stay-bright' buckle and fittings. The pouch, originally used to carry 20 rounds of ammunition and made of leather, is also made of thick black plastic with the regimental crest or cypher in the centre and now used to carry anything the bandsmen want to put in it. The waist belt and sword slings are also made of thick white plastic, with 'stay-bright' buckles and fittings.

The uniform of the Bandmaster is slightly different from those of the bandsmen and will be dealt with under the relevant regiment. However, it is the general rule that all Bandmasters are Warrant Officers Class 1 and they carry the standard pattern 1912 officers sword.

1st THE QUEEN'S DRAGOON GUARDS

BATTLE HONOURS

BLENHEIM	FRANCE AND FLANDERS 1914-18
RAMILLIES	
OUDENARDE	AFGHANISTAN 1919
MALPLAQUET	
DETTINGEN	SOMME 1940
WARBURG	BEDA FOMM
BEAUMONT	DEFENCE OF TOBRUK
WILLEMS	
WATERLOO	GAZALA
SEVASTOPOL	DEFENCE OF ALAMEIN LINE
LUCKNOW	
TAKU FORTS	EL ALAMEIN
PEKIN 1860	ADVANCE ON TRIPOLI
SOUTH AFRICA 1879	
SOUTH AFRICA 1901-2	TEBAGA GAP
	EL HAMMA
MONS	TUNIS
LE CATEAU	NORTH AFRICA 1941-3
MARNE 1914	
MESSINES 1914	MONT CAMINO
YPRES 1914, 1915	GOTHIC LINE
SOMME 1916, 1918	CORIANO
MORVAL	LAMONE CROSSING
SCARPE 1917	
CAMBRAI 1917, 1918	RIMINI LINE
AMIENS	ARGENTA GAP
PURSUIT TO MONS	ITALY 1943-4

Colonel-in-Chief
HM Queen Elizabeth the Queen Mother

Motto
Pro rege et patria (For King and Country)

History
Formed on 1 January 1959 by the amalgamation of the 1st King's Dragoon Guards and the 2nd Dragoon Guards (the Queen's Bays).

Home Headquarters
Maindy Barracks, Whitchurch Road, Cardiff CF4 3YE

Regimental Association
Maindy Barracks, Whitchurch Road, Cardiff CF4 3YE

Regimental Museum
Cardiff Castle, Cardiff, South Glamorgan

Marches

Quick march	Regimental march of the 1st The Queen's Dragoon Guards ('Radetsky' and 'Rusty Buckles')
Slow march	1st Dragoon Guards and 2nd Dragoon Guards march

Distinctions

The 1st The Queen's Dragoon Guards is the senior cavalry regiment of the British army, both former regiments having been raised in 1685.

In 1896 the Emperor Franz Joseph of Austria became the Colonel-in-Chief of the 1st King's Dragoon Guards and he bestowed upon the regiment the right to wear the 'Hapsburg double-headed eagle' as their cap badge. This honour is still evident today, having been continued after their amalgamation with the Queen's Bays.

There is a total of 46 battle honours emblazoned on the drums of the Regimental Band, thus bearing testimony to the many theatres of war the Regiment has participated in. During the Gulf War (1991) the 1st The Queen's Dragoon Guards formed the reconnaissance unit for the 7th Armoured Brigade (The Desert Rats), although the bandsmen were deployed as medics.

Bandsman

Yellow metal helmet with the number 1 on the front plate and a white plume.

The scarlet tunic has dark blue velvet collar, shoulder straps and cuffs. All the piping is yellow with the exception of the front edge of the tunic which is dark blue. The collar badges are 'staybright', but the shoulder titles and pouch cypher are of white metal. All chevrons are gold regimental lace on a dark blue backing.

Cavalry trousers are dark blue with a 1¾" white stripe down each outer seam.

Bandmaster

The uniform follows the same pattern as for the bandsmen with the following differences.

The helmet plume is scarlet.

All piping on the tunic is gold, with gold braid around the top of the collar. The epaulettes are made of gold interwoven cord. The pouch belt is of gold regimental lace with black leather backing and gilt fittings. The black leather pouch has a silver plate covering the top, engraved with the 'Hapsburg eagle' in the centre. Similarly the

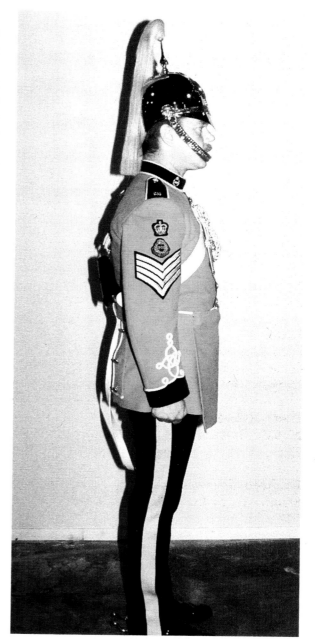

Trumpet Major, 1st The Queen's Dragoon Guards. Note the four chevrons on the upper half of his right arm. They are not inverted.

waist belt and sword slings are gold regimental lace with black leather backing and gilt fittings. A WO1 badge is worn above the cuff on the lower right sleeve.

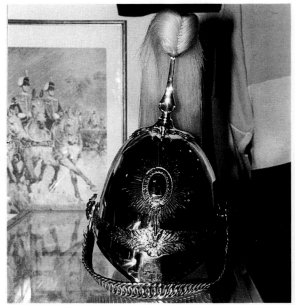

Above: *Front and rear view of the Bandmaster, in full ceremonial uniform.*

Right: *The metal helmet as worn by O/Rs. Note the white plume as opposed to the scarlet plume worn by the Bandmaster.*

THE ROYAL SCOTS DRAGOON GUARDS
(Carabiniers and Greys)

BATTLE HONOURS

BLENHEIM	ARRAS 1917
RAMILLIES	CAMBRAI 1917, 1918
OUDENARDE	SOMME 1918
MALPLAQUET	AMIENS
DETTINGEN	HINDENBURG LINE
WARBURG	CANAL DU NORD
BEAUMONT	
WILLEMS	PURSUIT TO MONS
TALAVERA	HILL 112
ALBUHERA	
VITTORIA	FALAISE
PENINSULA	HOCHWALD
WATERLOO	ALLER
BALAKLAVA	MERJAYUN
SEVASTOPOL	ALAM EL HALFA
DELHI 1857	EL ALAMEIN
ABYSSINIA	NOFILIA
AFGHANISTAN 1879-80	SALERNO
RELIEF OF KIMBERLEY	IMPHAL
PAARDEBURG	NUNSHIGUM
SOUTH AFRICA 1899-1902	BISHENPUR
	KANGLATONGBI
RETREAT FROM MONS	KENNEDY PEAK
MARNE 1914	SAGAING
AISNE 1914	MANDALAY
MESSINES 1914	AVA
YPRES 1914, 1915	IRRAWADDY

Colonel-in-Chief
HM The Queen

Motto
Second to none

History
Formed on 2 July 1971 by the amalgamation of the 2nd Dragoons (Royal Scots Greys) and the 3rd Carabiniers (Prince of Wales's Dragoon Guards).

Home Headquarters
The Castle, Edinburgh EM1 2YT, Scotland

Regimental Association
The Castle, Edinburgh EM1 2YT, Scotland

Regimental Museum
The Castle, Edinburgh EM1 2YT, Scotland

Marches
Band
Quick march   3rd Dragoon Guards
Slow march   'Garb of old Gaul'
Pipes & Drums
Quick march   'Hielan' Laddie'
Slow march   'My Home'
Combined Band & Pipes
Marches   'Scotland the Brave'
                'The Black Bear'

Walk	'Men of Harlech'
Trot	'Keel Row'
Canter	'Bonnie Dundee'

Regimental Mascot

A Drum Horse called 'Ramillies'

Distinctions

The earliest record of a regimental band dates from 1877, when for dismounted parades the trumpeters of The Scots Greys played on clarinets, bassoons and French horns. The 'Music Master' at this time was in all probability a civilian musician who was paid by the regiment to instruct them.

The famous white bearskin, worn by the Kettle Drummer, is unique in the British army and believed by many to have been presented by Tsar Alexander II of Russia in 1887 when he was the Colonel-in-Chief of the Scots Greys. However, there is some evidence that it was introduced as an experiment before this date. It is worn by the bass drummer when the drum horse is not on parade.

In 1972 the regimental band, together with the pipes and drums, made music history when it topped the charts worldwide with the hit single 'Amazing Grace'. To date the record has sold over 14 million copies!

There are a total of 51 battle honours emblazoned on the drums. This distinguished regiment, the only Cavalry regiment from Scotland, has served in all theatres of war from Blenheim to the Gulf, where they were part of the 7th Armoured Brigade (The Desert Rats). The band, taking on their secondary role as medics, treated numerous enemy casualties on route for Kuwait City as prisoners of war.

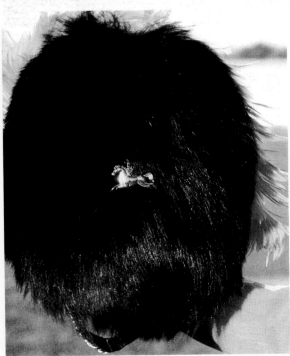

Above: *The bearskin worn by O/Rs in the Regimental Band of the Royal Scots Dragoon Guards. Note the 'flaming grenade' holder from which the scarlet hackle extends.* RSDG
Left: *The rear of the O/Rs bearskin showing the white metal 'Horse of Hanover'.* RSDG

Bandsman

The head-dress is a black fur bearskin with a large scarlet feather hackle crossing over the top from one side to the other. The hackle is held in place on the left side by a brass 'flaming grenade' plume holder. On the back of the bearskin is a white metal 'white horse of Hanover'. The chin-chains are brass on a black leather backing. The white bearskin of the kettle drummer has the same scarlet hackle and fittings.

The scarlet tunic follows the 'Dragoon' style with yellow collars, shoulder straps and cuffs. All piping is yellow and all badges worn are embroidered onto a dark blue backing, with the exception of the shoulder titles which are 'stay-bright'. The pouch is white with a gilt embroidered cypher (on dark blue backing) in the centre. All chevrons are gold regimental lace on yellow backing.

Left: *Detail of the Pipe Major's banner: the Royal Arms of Scotland on a royal blue background edged with a gold fronge.* RSDG
Right: *Insignia of rank of the Pipe Major: all badges are gold with the exception of the silver eagle on gold crossed carbines.* RSDG

The cavalry trousers are dark blue with two 1″ yellow stripes down each outer seam.

The kettle drummer and mounted trumpeters wear black knee high service boots with white metal box spurs.

Bandmaster

The uniform of the Bandmaster follows the same pattern as that for the bandsmen with the following exceptions.

The head-dress is the Guards Officers' pattern with the same accountrements.

The yellow collar is edged around the top in gold braid and all piping is gold. The epaulettes are made of gold interwoven cord, slightly thicker than the gold cord of the aiguillette. The pouch belt is of gold regimental lace, with black leather backing and gilt fittings. The black leather pouch has a silver plate on the front with a gilt eagle in the centre. Similarly the waist belt and sword slings are of gold regimental lace with black leather backing and gilt fittings. No badge of rank is worn.

Pipes and Drums

Piper

The head-dress is a black feather Highland bonnet with a white hackle on the left, held in place by a silver eagle plume holder. Around the rim is a yellow and dark blue 'Vandyke' pattern. The chin strap is black leather.

The single breasted doublet is dark blue with yellow piping and gold regimental lace on the wings. All buttons are silver. The kilt and plaid are the Royal Stuart tartan, the plaid being held in place by a silver 'white horse of Hanover' brooch. The cross belt and waist belt are black leather with silver buckles and fittings. By tradition all pipers wear a dirk on the right of

Left and centre: Drum Major, Pipes & Drums. Note his bearskin has a white plume on the left. RSDG
Right: Rear view of the Bass drummer. RSDG

their belt, a short dagger heavily embellished with black leather and silver. The sporran hangs on the front of the kilt from a chain to the waist. The richly engraved silver top supports the horse-hair plumes that cover the leather pouch beneath. The white horse-hair backing contrasts with the three red and black plumes.

The hose is red with brown criss-cross pattern, showing green diamonds where the brown lines cross. Yellow garter flashes are worn. The sgian dubh, or black knife, is carried in the top of the right hose. Although it was not traditionally part of the old Highland dress some references do relate a sleeve knife and it is generally accepted that the sgian dubh has evolved from that.

Shoes are black Highland pattern with white gaiters.

Pipe Major
The uniform is generally the same as the piper's with the following changes.

The Highland bonnet is slightly larger and fuller, with the same fittings.

The doublet has gold regimental lace around the top and bottom of the collar, the cuffs and cuff piping. The skirt flaps are heavily laced in gold. Badges of rank are worn on the right arm and the Pipe Major has the distinction of wearing the Regimental Dirk.

Drummers
The uniform is the same as for the bandsmen, however the bearskin is smaller and has a white hackle on the left side. The pouches are black.

Drum Major
The uniform is the same as the drummer's with the yellow piping being replaced by gold and the addition of dark blue wings laced in gold. Badges of rank are worn on the right arm and the Drum Major carries a standard pattern cavalry sword.

The dark blue sash is edged in gold lace and displays the regimental crests and battle honours. The mace is made of light ash and embellished with a gold chain, with a gold sleeve at the bottom and a gold carved head at the top.

Instruments
Although the regimental band use traditional drums with white metal tensions, the pipes and drums use the new fibreglass drums, with the bass drum having the regimental crests on the skins.

The pipe drones are draped with Royal Stuart tartan and Royal blue ribbons, with the bag being Royal Stuart. The pipes of the Pipe Major have the addition of a gold fringed banner displaying the regimental crest on one side and the Arms of Scotland on the other.

Bass Drummer of the Regimental Band wearing the white bearskin with the scarlet hackle. RSDG

13

Top: *One of a pair of Drum Banners carried by the Drum Horse. Gold and silver embroidery on a scarlet cloth with gold edging and fringe.*
Above: *The shabraque worn by the Drum Horse. It follows the same design and colours as the Drum Banners.* RSDG

Drum Horse

The Royal Scots Dragoon Guards have the distinction of being one of the three cavalry of the line regiments to have a drum horse. The present horse, a black stallion called 'Ramillies', was presented to the regiment in 1987 by HM The Queen at Windsor.

The harness is brown leather with gilt and steel fittings, with a black over red throat plume.

The saddle is covered by a black sheepskin. The shabraque is scarlet edged in gold lace and heavily embroidered with gold and silver wire in each corner.

The drum banners follow the same composition as the shabraque, with the addition of the battle honours and the cyphers of the former regimental connections in the four corners.

4th/7th ROYAL DRAGOON GUARDS

BATTLE HONOURS

BLENHEIM	YPRES 1914, 1915
RAMILLIES	SOMME 1916
OUDENARDE	AMIENS
MALPLAQUET	HINDENBURG LINE
DETTINGEN	PURSUIT TO MONS
WARBURG	DYLE
PENINSULA	DUNKIRK 1940
SOUTH AFRICA 1846-7	NORMANDY LANDING
BALAKLAVA	ODON
SEVASTOPOL	MONT PINÇON
TEL-EL-KEBIR	NEDERRIJN
EGYPT 1882	GEILENKIRCHEN
SOUTH AFRICA 1900-02	RHINELAND
MARNE 1914	CLEVE
AISNE 1914	RHINE
LA BASSÉE 1914	

Colonel-in-Chief
Hon Major-General HRH The Duchess of Kent GCVO

Motto
Quis separabit (Who shall separate us?)

History
Formed on 22 October 1922 as the 4th/7th Dragoon Guards by the amalgamation of the 4th Royal Irish Dragoon Guards and the 7th Dragoon Guards (Princess Royal's). The regiment was granted the prefix 'Royal' in October 1936.

Home Headquarters
3 Tower Street, York YO1 1SB

Regimental Association
3 Tower Street, York YO1 1SB

Regimental Museum
3 Tower Street, York YO1 1SB

Marches
Quick march	'St Patrick's Day'
Slow march	4th Dragoon's Slow March
	7th Dragoon's Slow March

One of a pair of silver kettle drums once carried by the regimental drum horse. 4th/7th RDG

Distinctions

Since 5 June 1945 (following an account in The Daily Telegraph) the 4th/7th Royal Dragoon Guards have been remembered for their nickname 'The First and Last'. In 1918 they were the first to cross the Hohenzollern Bridge over the Rhine in Germany. In 1939 they were the first (with their new tanks) to arrive in France with the BEF. In 1944 their specially water-proofed tanks were the first ashore in Normandy on D-Day. Finally, on 4 May 1945 (along with the 51st Highland Division) the 4th/7th Royal Dragoon Guards were the last British troops to see action against the Germans.

The 4th/7th Royal Dragoon Guards have a total of 31 battle honours emblazoned on their drums. In keeping with other regiments the bandsmen are deployed as medics in time of war, thus fulfilling their secondary role.

Bandsman

Yellow metal helmet with the number 4 on the front plate and a white plume.

The scarlet tunic has a dark blue collar, shoulder straps and cuffs. All piping is yellow with the exception of the front edge of the tunic which is dark blue. The collar badges are white metal with enamelled centres. The pouch is black with a white metal regimental cypher in the centre. A yellow aiguillette is worn on the left shoulder. No badges of rank are worn on the ceremonial uniform.

The cavalry trousers are dark blue with a 1¾" yellow stripe down each outer seam.

Detail of the insignia worn on the lower right sleeve of the Bandmaster.

Bandmaster

The uniform worn by the Bandmaster is the same as that worn by the bandsman with the following changes.

All piping is gold, the aiguillette is gold and the epaulettes are interwoven gold cord. The pouch belt is gold regimental lace on a dark blue leather backing with a gilt buckle and fittings, with the sword slings being the same. The black leather pouch has a silver top plate with a gold cypher in the centre. Contrary to the bandsmen, the Bandmaster does wear badges of rank on the lower right sleeve.

Top: The Regimental Band of the 4th/7th Royal Dragoon Guards in Germany. 4th/7th RDG
Far left and centre: The Bass Drummer, the front and rear views. Note the crests emblazoned on the drum. 4th/7th RDG
Left: The full ceremonial uniform as worn by the bandsmen.

5th ROYAL INNISKILLING DRAGOON GUARDS

BATTLE HONOURS

BLENHEIM	SOUTH AFRICA 1899-1902
RAMILLIES	
OUDENARDE	LE CATEAU
MALPLAQUET	MARNE 1914
DETTINGEN	SOMME 1916
WARBURG	CAMBRAI 1917
BEAUMONT	AMIENS
WILLEMS	HINDENBURG LINE
SALAMANCA	PURSUIT TO MONS
VITTORIA	WITHDRAWAL TO ESCAUT
TOULOUSE	
PENINSULA	ST OMER-LA-BASSÉE
WATERLOO	DUNKIRK 1940
BALAKLAVA	MONT PINÇON
SEVASTOPOL	LOWER MAAS
DEFENCE OF LADYSMITH	THE HOOK 1952
	KOREA 1951-2

Colonel-in-Chief
HRH The Prince of Wales KG, KT, GCB, AK, QSO, ADC

Motto
Vestigia nulle retrorsum (We do not retreat)

History
Formed in April 1922 as the 5th/6th Dragoons upon the amalgamation of the 5th Dragoon Guards (Princess Charlotte of Wales's) and The Inniskilling (6th Dragoons). Re-designated the 5th Inniskilling Dragoon Guards in May 1927 and granted the prefix 'Royal' in June 1935.

Home Headquarters
The Castle, Chester, Cheshire CH1 2DN

Regimental Association
The Castle, Chester, Cheshire CH1 2DN

Regimental Museum
The Castle, Chester, Cheshire CH1 2DN

Marches
Quick march	'Fare ye well Inniskilling'
Slow march	'The Soldier's Chorus' (from Gounod's *Faust*)

Opposite page: *Bandmasters in full ceremonial uniform. Left, 4th/7th Royal Dragoon Guards and right, 5th Royal Inniskilling Dragoon Guards, at the Royal Tournament in London 1991.*

Above: *Bandsman, 5th Royal Inniskilling Dragoon Guards. Note the shape of the helmet, the collar badge and the shoulder titles.*
Below: *Rear view of O/R's ceremonial uniform.*

Distinctions

A regiment's pride is not only enhanced by battles, but also by acts of individual heroism that reflect upon the regiment. On St Patrick's Day 1912, Captain L. Oates of the Inniskillings, terribly crippled by frostbite, left the safety of the tent and disappeared into a blizzard during Scott's Antarctic expedition. Rather than impede his comrades' progress any further, Oates then sacrificed himself to enable the remainder of the party to survive. Unfortunately his sacrifice was in vain.

The 5th Royal Inniskilling Dragoon Guards have 31 battle honours emblazoned on their drums. The most recent action seen by the regiment has been in the Gulf Conflict (1991), where two squadrons have remained to help in maintaining the status quo there.

Bandsman

Yellow metal helmet with the number 5 on the white metal front plate and a scarlet plume.

The scarlet tunic has a dark blue velvet collar, shoulder straps and cuffs. All piping is yellow with the exception of the front edge of the tunic which is dark blue. The collar badges are white metal 'Enniskillen Castles'. The pouch is black with a 'stay-bright castle' in the centre. All bandsmen wear gold aiguillettes on the left shoulder. The shoulder titles are 'stay-bright' and all chevrons are gold regimental lace.

The cavalry trousers are dark green with a 1¾" primrose stripe down each outer seam.

Bandmaster

The uniform is the same as for the bandsman with the following differences.

All piping is gold and the epaulettes are gold interwoven cord. The pouch belt, waist belt and sword slings are of gold regimental lace with a crimson line through the centre. All buckles and fittings are gilt. The pouch is of black leather with a silver top embellished by a silver 'castle' superimposed upon a gilt 'ER'. Badges of rank are worn on the lower right sleeve.

Full ceremonial uniform as worn by O/Rs.

Side drummer in full ceremonial uniform.

LANCERS

There are three regiments of Lancers in the British army today.
The 9th/12th Royal Lancers (Prince of Wales's)
The 16th/5th The Queen's Royal Lancers
The 17th/21st Lancers

The present uniform of Lancer regiments owes its origin to the Polish Lancers of Napoleon Bonaparte, who used them with such effectiveness that other European armies quickly formed their own, including the British.

The distinctive lancer cap or 'czapka', originally made of black leather (as the Bandmaster's still are), are now made of black fibreglass. The upper panels on top are covered in cloth of the regimental facing colour, piped yellow where the panels meet and edged in brass on the top corners. The front badge consists of brass rays with a white metal regimental crest in the centre. The brass chin-chain is held in place on either side by brass rosettes and a brass hook is on the rear of the cap to hold the chin-chain when it is not in use. Around the centre of the cap is lace of regimental colours over which the yellow cap lines pass before being attached to the tunic. The colours of the cockade, which has a brass regimental button in the centre, vary according to the regiment as do the plumes which fall from a holder just above the cockade.

The serge tunic has plain collars and cuffs in the regimental facing colour, with a double-breasted plastron on the front. All piping on the tunic is of the facing colour, with all buttons

Bandmaster of the 17th/21st Lancers at The Royal Tournament in London, 1991.

being 'stay-bright'. The yellow cap lines hang down at the back, passing through the right shoulder straps, across the body and back to the shoulder strap and across the body to the top left of the plastron, with the 'acorn' ends hanging down. The girdle is the same for all the lancer regiments with the only differences being those of the Bandmasters. These are yellow nylon with two scarlet stripes equally spaced running through. Pouch belts are of white plastic with black plastic pouches and white metal fittings.

The cavalry trousers are dark blue with two ¾" stripes on each outer seam. Short cavalry pattern boots are worn with white metal box spurs.

All Bandmasters are Warrant Officers Class 1 and carry the standard pattern 1912 officers sword.

Bandmasters of all three Lancer Regiments in full ceremonial uniform as they appeared at the Royal Tournament in London 1991. Left to right: 9th/12th Royal Lancers (POW); 16th/5th Queen's Royal Lancers; and 17th/21st Lancers.

9th/12th ROYAL LANCERS (PRINCE OF WALES'S)

Colonel-in-Chief
HM Queen Elizabeth the Queen Mother

Motto
The regiment does not have one

History
Formed on 11 September 1960 by the amalgamation of the 9th Queen's Royal Lancers and the 12th Royal Lancers (Prince of Wales's)

Home Headquarters
The TA Centre, Saffron Road, Wigston, Leicestershire

Regimental Association
The TA Centre, Saffron Road, Wigston, Leicestershire

Regimental Museum
Derby Museum and Art Gallery, The Strand, Derby

Marches
Quick march   'God Bless The Prince of Wales'
Slow march   'Men of Harlech'

BATTLE HONOURS

SALAMANCA
PENINSULA
WATERLOO
PUNNIAR
SOBRAON
CHILLIANWALLAH
GOOJERAT
PUNJAB
SOUTH AFRICA 1851-3
SEVASTOPOL
DELHI 1857
CENTRAL INDIA
LUCKNOW
CHARASIAH
KABUL 1879
KANDAHAR 1880
AFGHANISTAN 1878-80
MODDER RIVER
RELIEF OF KIMBERLEY
PAARDEBURG
SOUTH AFRICA 1899-1902
MONS
RETREAT FROM MONS
MARNE 1914
AISNE 1914

MESSINES 1914
YPRES 1914, 1915
SOMME 1916, 1918
ARRAS 1917
CAMBRAI 1917, 1918
ROSIÈRES
SAMBRE
PURSUIT TO MONS
DYLE
DUNKIRK 1940
SOMME 1940
NORTH-WEST EUROPE 1940
CHOR ES SUFAN
GAZALA
RUWEISAT
EL ALAMEIN
EL HAMMA
TUNIS
NORTH AFRICA 1941-3
DEFENCE OF LAMONE BRIDGEHEAD
ARGENTA GAP
BOLOGNA
ITALY 1944-5

Distinctions

This is the oldest of the Lancer regiments with the 12th Royal Lancers being formed in 1817 and the 9th Queen's Royal Lancers being formed in 1822. The band play regimental hymns twice a week at their memorial. These hymns were presented to the 12th Royal Lancers by Pope Pius VI, who was most impressed by the regiment's good conduct during their stay in Italy in 1793.

The 9th/12th Royal Lancers (POW) have been in the forefront of all the major actions engaged by the British army, as their 48 battle honours emblazoned on their drums testify. During the Gulf War (1991) the band was stationed at Bulford as a medical post to receive casualties as a result of the war. Luckily their services were not required!

Right: Fanfare Trumpeter in full ceremonial uniform.
Right: The fanfare trumpet banner. The crest is embroidered onto a scarlet cloth with a gold fringe.
Below:Bass drum. All cyphers are on a scarlet shell.

Bandsman

The upper panels of the lance cap are scarlet, with the top (or mortar-board) black. The lace around the centre of the cap is white with a dark blue band through the middle. The cockade on the left is dark blue edged with white. The plume is scarlet.

The dark blue tunic has scarlet collars, cuffs, plastron and piping. The shoulder cords are yellow and all chevrons are gold regimental lace on scarlet backing.

Bandmaster

As for the uniform of the bandsman with the following differences.

The upper panels and top of the lance cap are scarlet, with all piping gold (this crosses over the top) and gold braid on the peak. The lace around the centre of the cap is gold with a dark blue band through the middle. Gold cap lines.

The tunic has gold lace around the collar and cuffs, with gold interwoven cord epaulettes. The pouch belt is gold regimental lace with red leather backing and gilt fittings. The pricker and chains on the front are silver. The red leather pouch has a gilt covered top with the regimental cypher in the centre. The girdle is gold lace with two scarlet lines running through it, equally spaced. The sword slings are the same as the pouch belt, with gilt fittings. Badges of rank are worn on the lower right sleeve.

9th/12th Royal Lancers (POW) on parade.

16th/5th THE QUEEN'S ROYAL LANCERS

BATTLE HONOURS

BLENHEIM
RAMILLIES
OUDENARDE
MALPLAQUET
BEAUMONT
WILLEMS
TALAVERA
FUENTES D'ONOR
SALAMANCA
VITTORIA
NIVE
PENINSULA
WATERLOO
BHURTPORE
GHUZNEE 1839
AFGHANISTAN 1839
MAHARAJPORE
ALIWAL
SOBRAON
SUAKIN 1885
DEFENCE OF
   LADYSMITH
RELIEF OF
   KIMBERLEY
PAARDEBURG
SOUTH AFRICA 1899-1902
MONS

LE CATEAU
RETREAT FROM
   MONS
MARNE 1914
AISNE 1914
MESSINES 1914
YPRES 1914, 1915
BELLEWAARDE
ARRAS 1917
CAMBRAI 1917
SOMME 1918
ST QUENTIN
PURSUIT TO
   MONS
FONDOUK
BORDJ
DJEBEL
   KOURNINE
TUNIS
NORTH AFRICA
   1942-3
CASSINO II
LIRI VALLEY
ADVANCE TO
   FLORENCE
ARGENTA GAP
ITALY 1944-5

Colonel-in-Chief
HM The Queen

Motto
Aut cursu aut cominus armis (Either in the charge or hand to hand)

History
Formed in April 1922 as the 16th/5th Lancers by the amalgamation of the 16th The Queen's Lancers and the 5th Royal Irish Lancers. Redesignated as the 16th/5th The Queen's Royal Lancers on 16 June 1954.

Home Headquarters
Kitchener House, Lammascote Road, Stafford ST16 3TA

Regimental Association
Kitchener House, Lammascote Road, Stafford ST16 3TA

Regimental Museum
Kitchener House, Lammascote Road, Stafford ST16 3TA

Marches
Quick march   'Scarlet and Green'
Slow march   'The Queen Charlotte'

The Regimental Band performing at a festival in Germany.   16th/5th QRL

The bass drum. The crests are on a scarlet shell.
16th/5th QRL

Distinctions

Affectionately known as the 'Scarlet Lancers', the 16th Queen's Lancers have distinguished themselves repeatedly during Britain's many conflicts, including their famous charge at Aliwal. The regimental guidon, presented by HM The Queen in March 1959, bears Her Majesty's personal cypher, a rare distinction for any British regiment.

The drums of the regimental band bear 47 battle honours. During the Gulf War (1991) the regiment was deployed as the medium reconnaissance unit for the 1st (British) Armoured Division, leading the Division though the breach in Iraqi defences to advance some 45 miles into Iraq before turning east towards Northern Kuwait. The bandsmen gave their support to this operation by reverting to their secondary role as medics.

Bandsman

The upper panels of the lance cap are dark blue, with a black top. The lace around the centre of the cap is yellow with with a single scarlet line through the middle. The cockade is scarlet, circled by three bands – yellow, scarlet, yellow. The plume is black.

The scarlet tunic has a dark blue collar, cuffs, plastron and piping. The shoulder cords are yellow. All chevrons are gold on a scarlet backing.

The cavalry trousers are dark blue with two ¾″ yellow stripes down each outer seam.

Bandmaster

The upper panels and top of the lance cap are dark blue, with all piping gold (this crosses over the top) and heavy gold braid on the peak. Gold cap lines.

The remainder of the uniform is the same as that for the bandsman with the following differences.

The collar and cuffs are laced with gold braid and the piping on the rear of the skirt is gold. The shoulder cords are interwoven gold cords. The girdle is regimental lace with a single yellow line through the centre. The pouch belt and sword slings are gold regimental lace with a dark blue line running through the centre and backed with dark blue leather. All buckles and fittings are gilt. The prickers and chain on the front of the pouch belt are silver and the top of the pouch is silver with a gilt regimental cypher in the centre. Badges of rank are worn on the lower right sleeve.

Fanfare Trumpet Banner. The cypher is embroidered onto a scarlet cloth with gold edging and fringe.
16th/5th QRL

O/R's full ceremonial uniform, rear and front view.
16th/5th QRL

17th/21st LANCERS

Colonel-in-Chief
HRH Princess Alexandra, The Hon Lady Ogilvy
GCVO

Motto
'Or Glory'

History
Formed in April 1922 by the amalgamation of
the 17th Lancers (Duke of Cambridge's Own)
and the 21st Lancers (Empress of India's).

Home Headquarters
Prince William of Gloucester Barracks, Grantham, Lincs

Regimental Association
Prince William of Gloucester Barracks, Grantham, Lincs

Regimental Museum
Belvoir Castle, Near Grantham, Lincolnshire

Marches
Quick march   'The White Lancer'
Slow march   'Rienzi'

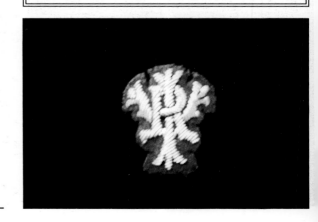

*Detail of the unique badge worn on the upper left
arm.*

Distinctions

After relaying the news of Wolfe's victory at Quebec, Lt Colonel John Hale was commissioned by the King to raise a Regiment of cavalry. Thus, on 7 November 1759 the 18th Light Dragoons (the founder regiment) were born. Hale intended the Regiment to be a memorial to Wolfe and chose the Death's Head as its badge with the motto 'Or Glory'. Since the two are inseparable parts of the full motto 'Death or Glory', it is referred to as the Regimental Motto and never as its badge.

Famous for their gallant charge with the Light Brigade at Balaklava in 1854 and for their part in the ultimate defeat of the Zulus at Ulundi in 1879, the 17th Lancers have had their share of 'glory'. Not to be outdone, the charge of the 21st Lancers against the Dervishes at Omdurman has also been immortalisd in history. The regimental drums depict this glorious past with 29 battle honours borne on them. More recently, the regi-

O/R's Lancer cap. Note the silver motto superimposed on brass rays.

ment has seen action in the Gulf War (1991) where the bandsmen served as medics under the 1st Armoured Field Ambulance.

Bandsman

The upper panels and top of the lance cap are white. The centre band is yellow with a French grey line running through the middle. The cockade is French grey with a yellow outer ring and the plume is white.

The dark blue tunic has white collar, cuffs, plastron and piping. The 17th/21st Lancers do

Detail of the Band Sgt/Major's insignia of rank. In this case a gold crown (WO2) and laurel leaves on a white backing. Below a silver embroiderd motto.

not wear a pouch or pouch belt. However, they do wear a small embroidered badge on the upper left arm, the cypher of Queen Victoria, 'VRI' on French grey backing. All chevrons are gold on white backing.

The cavalry trousers are dark blue with two ¾" white stripes down each outer seam.

Bandmaster

The uniform is the same as for the bandsman with the following differences.

The centre band of the lance cap is gold with a French grey line through the middle. The peak has gold braid across it and the cap lines are gold.

The collar and cuffs of the tunic are edged with gold braid and the epaulettes are made of interwoven gold cord. The waist belt is gold regimental lace with a centre line of yellow. The pouch belt is gold regimental lace with a white line through the centre and silver prickers and chains on the front. All buckles and fittings are white metal and the pouch has a silver top with a gilt cypher in the centre. The sword slings follow the same pattern as the pouch belt. All badges of rank are worn on the lower right sleeve.

Rear view of the Bandmaster's uniform.

Fanfare Trumpet Banner. The devices are embroidered on a dark blue backing. 17th/21st L

CONTINUED ON PAGE 4

CAVALRY
IN COLOUR

Below: *Pipe Major, Pipes & Drums.* RSDG

Above: *Drum Horse 'Ramillies', Royal Scots Dragoon Guards.* RSDG

Centre panel of bass drum, Pipes & Drums. RSDG

Side Drum, 1st The Queen's Dragoon Guards.

Side Drum, Royal Scots Dragoon Guards. RSDG

Side Drum, 4th/7th Royal Dragoon Guards.
4th/7th RDG

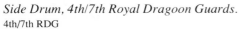

Side Drum, 5th Royal Inniskilling Dragoon Guards.

Side Drum, 9th/12th Royal Lancers, (POW).

Side Drum, 16th/5th The Queens Royal Lancers.
16th/5th QRL

Side Drum, 17th/21st Lancers.

Trumpet Banner of The Duke of Westminster, Colonel of the 9th/12th Royal Lancers (Prince of Wales's).

BANDMASTERS OF THE CAVALRY REGIMEN
From
Tank Regiment; 17th/21st Lancers; 15th/19th King's Royal Hussars; 13th
4th/7th Royal Dragoon Guards; 1st The Queen's Dragoon Guards; Director of
5th Royal Inniskilling Dragoon Guards; Queen's Roya
16th/15th Queen's Re

THE ROYAL TOURNAMENT IN LONDON 1991

ght:

al Hussars QMO; 9th/12th Royal Lancers POW; Queens Own Hussars;
ermany); Director of Music, Blues and Royals; Royal Scots Dragoon Guards;
ssars; The Royal Hussars; 14th/20th King's Hussars;
ers; Tank Regiment.

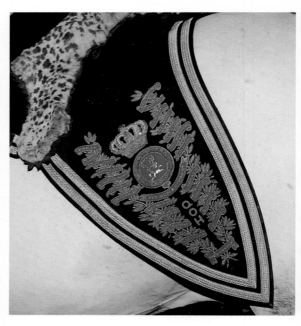

Left: *Drum Horse 'Dettingen', Queen's Own Hussars.*

Below left: *Detail of Drum Horse shabraque (front), QOH.*

Above: *Detail of Drum Horse Shabraque (rear), QOH.*

Below: *Side Drum, Queen's Own Hussars.*

Above: *Drum Horse 'Winston', Queen's Royal Irish Hussars.*

Above right: *Detail of Drum Horse shabraque, Queen's Royal Irish Hussars.*

Right: *Pipe Major, Queen's Royal Irish Hussars.*

Below: *Side Drum, Queen's Royal Irish Hussars.*

Above: Side Drum, The Royal Hussars.

Right: Side Drum, 13th/18th Royal Hussars, QMO.

Above: Side Drum, 14th/20th King's Hussars.

Right: Side Drum, 15th/19th King's Royal Hussars.
15th/19th KRH

The Regimental Band on parade. Note the absence of pouch belts, except for the Bandmaster.   17th/21st L

Detail of the chrevrons, all are of gold regimental lace on a white backing. From corporal upwards all chevrons have a silver embroidered motto in the centre, as shown here.

HUSSARS

At present there are six regiments of Hussars in the British army.

The Queen's Own Hussars
The Queen's Royal Irish Hussars
The Royal Hussars
13th/18th Royal Hussars (Queen Mary's Own)
14th/20th King's Hussars
15th/19th The King's Royal Hussars

Hussars were originally Light Cavalry used for scouting and the present uniform has been derived from the original 15th century Hungarian Light Horse Corps, the forerunners of the European Hussar regiments. Although the dolman (or pelisse) has now been discarded, the uniform of the British hussar regiments is basically the same.

The hussar cap is more popularly known as a 'busby' after the London hatter who supplied them, W. Busby of the Strand. Originally made of fur (as the Bandmasters still are) they are now made of black nylon fur and are cylindrical in shape with a cloth bag (or fly), drawn from the inside to hang down the right side. The colour of the fly varies according to the regiment, but they are all piped yellow. Yellow cap lines are drawn around the centre of the busby, from one side of the fly to the other, and then loop down to the tunic. On the front a yellow cord button is situated just below the plume holder. The colours of the plume vary according to the regiment. A brass chin-chain is suspended from the inside of the busby at either side.

The tunics of the hussars are all the same with only the colours of the collars varying according to the regiment. The tunic is dark blue serge with yellow piping top and bottom of the collar, along the edges of the tunic and around the cuffs, where the piping forms an 'Austrian knot'. The front has six rows of yellow cord with loops at each end known as 'frogging'. The rear has two rows of curved yellow cord with loops at each end. All buttons are 'stay-bright', with six on the front and two on the back. Pouch belts, originally made of leather, are now made of white plastic and the pouches can be either white or black. All fittings are of white metal.

With the exception of the Royal Hussars, all the cavalry trousers are dark blue with two ¾" stripes down each outer seam.

The short pattern cavalry boot is worn with white metal box spurs.

The uniform of the Bandmaster will be dealt with under the appropriate regimental heading, however they are all Warrant Officers Class 1 and they all carry the 1912 Officers pattern cavalry sword.

Above: *Bandmasters in full ceremonial uniform.*
Left: *15th/19th Kings's Royal Hussar and* right: 13th/18th Royal Hussars. QMO
Opposite: *A rear view of some Hussar Bandmasters at the Royal Tournament in London, 1991.*

THE QUEEN'S OWN HUSSARS

Colonel-in-Chief
HM Queen Elizabeth the Queen Mother

Motto
Nec aspera terrent (Nor do difficulties deter)

History
Formed on 3 November 1958 by the amalgamation of the 3rd the King's Own Hussars and the 7th Queen's Own Hussars.

Home Headquarters
28 Jury Street, Warwick, Warwickshire CV34 4EW

Regimental Association
28 Jury Street, Warwick, Warwickshire CV34 4EW

Regimental Museum
Lord Leicester Hospital, High Street, Warwick, Warwickshire

Marches

Quick march	(Regimental) Light Cavalry 'Robert the Devil' 'Bannocks of Barley Meal' (Inspection) 'The Dettingen March'
Slow march	The 3rd Hussars Slow March 'The Garb of Old Gaul'
Trot	'Encore'
Gallop	'The Campbells are Coming'

BATTLE HONOURS

DETTINGEN	CAMBRAI 1917, 1918
WARBURG	
BEAUMONT	SOMME 1918
WILLEMS	AMIENS
SALAMANCA	FRANCE AND FLANDERS 1914-18
VITTORIA	
ORTHES	KHAN BAGHDADI
TOULOUSE	SHARQAT
PENINSULA	MESOPOTAMIA 1917-18
WATERLOO	
CABOOL 1842	EGYPTIAN FRONTIER 1940
MOODKEE	
FEROZESHAH	BUQ BUQ
SOBRAON	BEDA FOMM
CHILLIANWALLAH	SIDI REZEGH 1941
GOOJERAT	EL ALAMEIN
PUNJAB	NORTH AFRICA 1940-2
LUCKNOW	
SOUTH AFRICA 1901-2	CITTA DELLA PIAVE
RETREAT FROM MONS	ANCONA
	ITALY 1944-5
MARNE 1914	CRETE
YPRES 1914, 1915	BURMA 1942

Opposite page
Left: *Rear view of Bandmaster's uniform.*
Centre top: *Bass drum. The shell is a rich deep red.*
Centre below: *O/R's Busby.*
Right top: *The Bandmaster's uniform, front view.*
Right below: *Detail of NCO chevrons with the silver Regimental cypher above.*

The Drum Horse, shown without drums so the front part of the saddle can be seen.
Below left: *One of a pair of silver drums carried by the Drum horse. The Queen's Own Hussars do not have drum banners, battle honours are engraved on the drums.*
Below right: *Detail of the shabraque worn by the Drum horse. The gold embroidery is on a dark blue cloth with gold braid around the edges.*

Opposite page
Escort in full ceremonial uniform. Two escorts walk in front of the Drum horse with drawn swords, whenever the Drum horse is on parade.

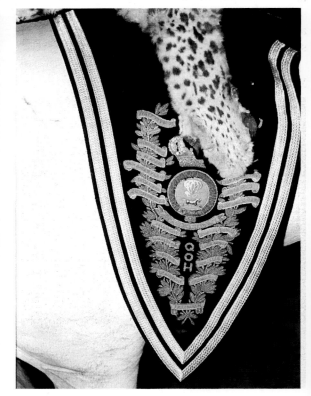

Regimental Mascot

A drum horse called 'Dettingen'.

Distinctions

The Queen's Own Hussars are the senior Hussar regiment of the British army.

The regiment is unique in the fact that they do not have drum banners. The battle honours are borne on the silver drums captured at the Battle of Dettingen in 1743.

The Kettle Drummer wears a 3¾″ high silver collar, presented to the 3rd King's Own Hussars in 1772 by the wife of Lord Southampton upon the appointment of her husband as Colonel of the regiment.

There are a total of 40 battle honours engraved on the silver drums, depicting the gallantry displayed over the years in all theatres of war.

Bandsman

The busby has a garter blue fly with yellow piping and a white plume.

The tunic has a scarlet collar and the pouch at the rear is black. All chevrons are gold on scarlet backing.

The dark blue cavalry trousers have two ¾″ yellow stripes down each outer seam.

Bandmaster

The uniform for the Bandmaster is the same as that for the bandsman with the following differences.

All piping on the busby and the cap lines are gold.

All piping, frogging and loops on the tunic are gold. The epaulettes are of gold interwoven cord. The pouch belt and sword slings are of gold regimental lace backed with scarlet leather. The pouch is scarlet leather, heavily embellished with gold inlays of leaves with a gilt cypher in the centre. All fittings are white metal. No badges of rank are worn.

Drum Horse

The present drum horse, 'Dettingen', is a white stallion and was presented to the regiment by HM Queen Elizabeth the Queen Mother.

All harnessing is dark brown leather, with the exception of the head bands and chest straps which are pale blue leather. All fittings are gilt and steel. The saddle is covered with a leopard skin backed with garter blue cloth. The shabraque is dark blue with two lines of gold braid around the edge. All the embroidery is of gold and silver wire. The throat plume is white.

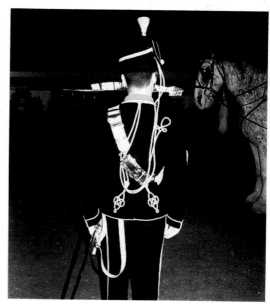

THE QUEEN'S ROYAL IRISH HUSSARS

Colonel-in-Chief
Field Marshal HRH The Prince Philip, Duke of Edinburgh KG, KT, OM, GBE, AC, QSO

Motto
Mente et manu (With heart and hand)
Pristinae virtutis memores (The memory of former valour)

History
Formed on 24 October 1958 by the amalgamation of the 4th Queen's Own Hussars and the 8th (King's Royal Irish) Hussars.

Home Headquarters
Regent's Park Barracks, Albany Street, London NW1

Regimental Association
Regent's Park Barracks, Albany Street, London NW1

Regimental Museums
Museum of Irish Cavalry Regiments, Carrickfergus, Co Antrim
Combined Services Museum, The Redoubt Fortress, Royal Parade, Eastbourne, East Sussex

Marches
Quick march   'St Patrick's Day'
                'Berkeley's Dragoons'
                'A Galloping 8th Hussar'

BATTLE HONOURS

DETTINGEN	BAPAUME 1918
LESWARREE	ROSIÈRES
HINDOOSTAN	AMIENS
TALAVERA	ALBERT 1918
ALBUHERA	BEAUREVOIR
SALAMANCA	PURSUIT TO MONS
VITTORIA	FRANCE AND
TOULOUSE	FLANDERS 1914-18
PENINSULA	VILLERS BOCAGE
GHUZNEE 1839	LOWER MAAS
AFGHANISTAN	ROER
1839	RHINE
ALMA	NORTH WEST
BALAKLAVA	EUROPE 1944-5
INKERMAN	BUQ BUQ
SEVASTOPOL	SIDI REZEGH 1941
CENTRAL INDIA	GAZALA
AFGHANISTAN	RUWEISAT
1879-80	ALAM EL HALFA
SOUTH AFRICA	EL ALAMEIN
1900-2	NORTH AFRICA
MONS	1940-2
LE CATEAU	CORIANO
MARNE 1914	SENIO POCKET
AISNE	RIMINI LINE
YPRES 1914, 1915	ARGENTA GAP
GIVENCHY 1914	PROASTEION
ST JULIEN	CORINTH CANAL
SOMME 1916, 1918	GREECE 1941
ARRAS 1917	IMJIN
CAMBRAI 1917,	KOREA 1950-1
1918	

Far left: *Detail of Bandmaster's pouch. Compare it with the O/R's pouch shown above.*
Centre: *Trumpet Major. Note the inverted gold chevrons on lower arm.*
Above: *Detail of O/R's pouch.*

Slow march   'Loretto'
                  'March of the Scottish Archers'

Regimental Mascot
A drum horse called 'Winston'

Distinctions
Both of the former regiments rode beside each other at the Charge of the Light Brigade in 1854.

More recently pipes have been added to the regimental band, with the pipers being selected from the trained armoured troops unlike the bandsmen whose secondary roles are as medics. The first official appearance of the pipes was on St Patrick's Day 1987 and since then have become a regular feature with the band.

There are no less than 56 battle honours borne on the regimental drums, the highest amount for any line cavalry regiment and a true testimony to the bravery of the regiment. During the Gulf War (1991) the regiment served as part of the 7th Armoured Brigade (The Desert Rats), with the band providing the medical services.

Bandsman
The busby has a yellow fly with yellow piping and a white over red plume.

The tunic has a dark blue collar and cuffs. The pouch is black. All chevrons are gold on scarlet backing, with Lance Corporals having two chevrons and Corporals also having two chevrons but with a white metal 'Irish harp' above.

The dark blue cavalry trousers have two ¾" yellow stripes down each outer seam.

Bandmaster
The uniform for the Bandmaster is the same as for the bandsman with the following differences.

All piping on the busby and tunic is gold, with gold cap lines. The pouch belt and sword slings are of gold regimental lace with a scarlet line through the centre and red leather backing. All fittings are white metal, but the prickers and chain on the pouch belt is silver. The pouch is red leather heavily embellished with gold scrolls, oak leaves and regimental cypher. No rank insignia is worn.

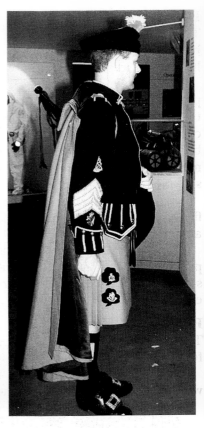

Top left: *The Bandmaster in full ceremonial uniform.*

Top centre: *Left side view of Bandmaster. Note the standard pattern 1912 sword.*

Top right: *Pipe Major. Insignia gold pipes above gold chevrons. Silver Irish Harp below.*

Left: *Bass drum. Gold cyphers on a dark green shell.*

Opposite page: *Fixing the drums on the Drum horse at the Royal Tournament, 1991.*

Piper

The caubeen is dark green with a 'stay-bright' badge on the front from which the white over red hackle emerges.

The single breasted, dark green tunic is piped yellow. All buttons are 'stay-bright' but the collar badges are white metal regimental cyphers. The belt is black with a 'stay-bright' buckle and the sporran is also black with a white metal 'Irish harp' on the front. The kilt is saffron.

The hose is dark green with saffron garter flashes. Black leather brogues with silver buckles are worn.

Pipers normally wear a cloak when on parade. This is saffron lined with dark green satin. The deep collar has gold braid around the edge.

Pipe Major

The uniform is the same as the piper's with the following difference.

All piping is gold and the rank insignia is worn on the right sleeve above the cuff.

Bagpipes

The bag is made of black velvet and the drones have dark green tassels and ribbons suspended from them.

Drum Horse

'Winston' (named after Sir Winston Churchill who was a Lieutenant in the 4th Hussars), was presented to the regiment by HRH Prince Philip at the Redoubt Museum, Eastbourne in July 1990. He is a large Clydesdale and the first drum horse the regiment has had since before 1939.

All of the harnessing is black leather with gilt and steel fittings. The saddle is covered by a leopardskin and the shabraque, originally of the 4th Hussars, is dark blue with gold braid and embroidery. The drum banners also date from before the Second World War. On the right is carried the crimson banner of the 8th King's Royal Irish Hussars and on the left is carried the yellow banner of the 4th Queen's Own Hussars. The throat plume is white emerging from scarlet.

Top left: *Detail of harness on Drum horse.*

Bottom left: *Detail of shabraque worn by the Drum horse. All cyphers gold on dark blue backing.*

Below: *Strapping on the banners at the 1991 Royal Tournament.*

Opposite page:
Above and below: *Detail of the two Drum Banners.*

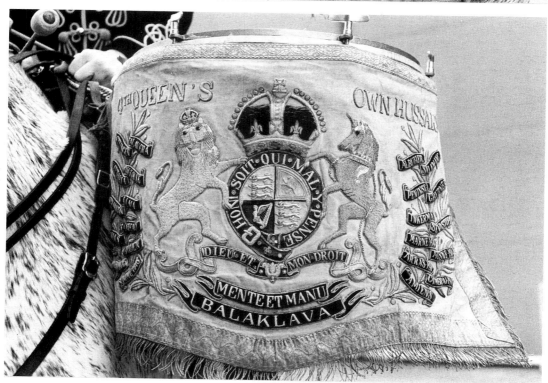

THE ROYAL HUSSARS

Colonel-in-Chief
HRH Princess Alice, Duchess of Gloucester
GCB, CI, GCVO, GBE

Motto
Ich dien (I serve)

History
Formed on 25 October 1969 by the amalgamation of the 10th Royal Hussars (Prince of Wales's Own) and the 11th Hussars (Prince Albert's Own).

Home Headquarters
Peninsular Barracks, Winchester, Hampshire

Regimental Association
Peninsular Barracks, Winchester, Hampshire

Regimental Museum
Peninsular Barracks, Winchester, Hampshire

Marches
Quick march   'The Merry Month of May'
Slow march   'Coburg'

BATTLE HONOURS

WARBURG
BEAUMONT
WILLEMS
SALAMANCA
PENINSULA
WATERLOO
BHURTPORE
ALMA
BALAKLAVA
INKERMAN
SEVASTOPOL
ALI MASJID
AFGHANISTAN 1878-9
EGYPT 1884
RELIEF OF KIMBERLEY
PAARDEBURG
SOUTH AFRICA 1899-1902
LE CATEAU
RETREAT FROM MONS
MARNE 1914
AISNE 1914
MESSINES 1914
FREZENBERG
LOOS
SOMME 1916, 1918
ARRAS 1917, 1918
CAMBRAI 1917, 1918

AMIENS
DROCOURT-QUEANT
SELLE
PURSUIT TO MONS
FRANCE AND FLANDERS 1914-18
SOMME 1940
VILLERS BOCAGE
ROER
RHINE
NORTH-WEST EUROPE 1940, 1944-5
EGYPTIAN FRONTIER 1940
SIDI BARRANI
BEDA FOMM
SIDI FEZEGH 1941
SAUNNU
GAZALA
EL ALAMEIN
EL HAMMA
TUNIS
CORIANO
SANTARCANGELO
VALLI DI COMACCHIO
ARGENTA GAP
ITALY 1943-5

Right: *Bass Drummer in full ceremonial uniform.*

Far right: *Detail of the rear of the bass Drummer, showing the leopard's head.*

Below: *The Regimental Band in Germany.* RH

Left: *Side drummer.*
Bottom left: *Fanfare trumpeter.*
Right: *Regimental drum, gold cyphers on crimson shell.*
Bottom right: *Fanfare trumpet banner. Gold and silver cyphers on a crimson banner.*

Distinctions

The 10th Royal Hussars (POW), nicknamed the 'Shiny Tenth' from their chain pounch belt, was the first British regiment to become hussars in 1806.

The 11th Hussars (PAO), nicknamed the 'Cherrypickers' from being caught in a cherry orchard during the Peninsular War, are famous for their part in the Charge of the Light Brigade under their Commanding Officer, Lord Cardigan.

Following their amalgamation, the Royal Hussars were the first regiment to be equipped with the new Challenger Main Battle tanks in 1983.

There are a total of 51 battle honours emblazoned on the regimental drums.

Bandsman

The busby has a scarlet fly with yellow piping, although to follow in line with the colours of the regiment it should be crimson. The plume is white over scarlet (again this should be crimson).

The tunic has a dark blue collar and cuffs. The pouch is black and all chevrons are gold on crimson backing.

The cavalry trousers are crimson with two 3/4" yellow stripes down each outer seam.

Bandmaster

The Bandmaster's uniform is the same as that for the bandsman with the following differences.

The busby fly is crimson with all piping and cap lines gold.

All piping, frogging and loops on the tunic are gold. The epaulettes are of gold interwoven cord. The pouch belt and sword slings are gold regimental lace backed with crimson leather. All fittings are white metal, except for the prickers and chain on the pouch belt which are silver. The pouch is crimson leather heavily embellished with gold oak leaves and a gilt cypher in the centre. No badges of rank are worn.

Front and rear view of the bandmaster in full ceremonial uniform.

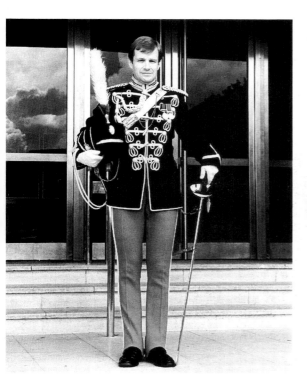
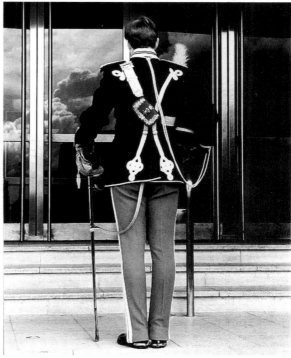

13th/18th ROYAL HUSSARS QUEEN MARY'S OWN

Colonel-in-Chief
HRH The Prince of Wales KG, KT, GCB, AK, QSO, ADC

Motto
Viret in aeternum (It shall flourish for ever)
Pro rege, pro lege, pro patria conamur (We strive for our King, our Law and our Country)

History
Formed in April 1922 as the 13th/18th Hussars by the amalagamation of the 13th Hussars and the 18th Royal Hussars (Queen Mary's Own). Re-designated the 13th/18th Royal Hussars (Queen Mary's Own) in December 1935.

Regimental Headquarters
3 Tower Street, York YO1 1SB

Regimental Association
3 Tower Street, York YO1 1SB

Regimental Museum
Cannon Hall, Barnsley, South Yorkshire

Marches
Quick march	'Balaklava'
Slow march	13th Hussars Slow March
	18th Hussars Slow March

BATTLE HONOURS

ALBUHERA	HINDENBURG LINE
VITTORIA	FRANCE AND
ORTHES	FLANDERS 1914-18
TOULOUSE	KUT AL AMARA 1917
PENINSULA	BAGHDAD
ALMA	SHARQAT
BALAKLAVA	MESOPOTAMIA
SEVASTOPOL	1916-18
DEFENCE OF	YPRES-COMINES
LADYSMITH	CANAL
SOUTH AFRICA	NORMANDY
1899-1902	LANDING
MONS	CAEN
MARNE 1914	MONT PINÇON
AISNE 1914	GEILENKIRCHEN
MESSINES 1914	ROER
YPRES 1915, 1916	RHINELAND
SOMME 1916, 1918	GOCH
CAMBRAI 1917,	NORTH-WEST
1918	EUROPE 1940,
AMIENS	1944-5

Opposite page:
Top left: *Fanfare Trumpeter.*
Top right: *Fanfare Trumpet Banner. Gold and white devices on a scarlet background.*
Below: *The Dance Band in mess dress.*
14th/18th RH (QMO)

Distinctions

The Band of the 13th Hussars can be traced back to 1814 when they were known as the 13th Light Dragoons, although there is no exact record of how many musicians it comprised of. However, official regimental records of 1823 do show that the band had one Sergeant-Master and 14 musicians.

The regimental drums display 33 battle honours from their pevious engagements, their latest engagement being their participation in the Gulf War (1991), where the band formed part of the 1st Armoured Field Ambulance during Operation Desert Storm.

Bandsman

The busby has a white fly with yellow piping, and a white plume.

The tunic has a white collar and the pouch is black. All chevrons are gold on a white backing.

The cavalry trousers are dark blue with two ¾" white stripes down each outer seam.

Bandmaster

The Bandmaster's uniform is the same as that for the bandsman with the following differences.

All piping on the busby and the cap lines are gold.

All piping, frogging and loops on the tunic are gold. The pouch belt and sword slings are gold regimental lace with a white line thorugh the centre. All fittings are white metal with the exception of the prickers and chain which are silver. The black pouch has a silver top with a gilt cypher in the centre. The epaulettes are of gold interwoven cord and all rank insignia is worn on the lower right sleeve.

This page
Top left: *Bass drummer with drums on parade in blues.*

Above: *The band in 'blues', Teignmouth, S. Devon 1990.*

Bottom left: *Trumpet Major in 'blues'.*

Opposite page:
Left: *The BSM in full ceremonial dress.*

Right: *Bass Drum. Gold and blue cyphers on white background.*

14th/20th KING'S HUSSARS

Colonel-in-Chief
HRH The Princess Royal GCVO

Motto
The regiment does not have one

History
Formed in April 1922 by the amalgamation of the 14th King's Hussars and the 20th Hussars as the 14th/20th Hussars. Re-designated the 14th/20th King's Hussars in December 1936.

Regimental Headquarters
Fulwood Barracks, Preston, Lancashire PR2 4AA

Regimental Association
Fulwood Barracks, Preston, Lancashire PR2 4AA

Regimental Museum
County and Regimental Museum, Stanley Street, Preston

Marches
Quick march 'Royal Sussex'
Slow march 'The Eagle'

Detail of the Prussian Eagle on the top of the bell lyre.

Opposite page:
Left: *Musician with bell lyre. The tassles are lilac and yellow.*
Right: *Bass Drummer. The shell is pale yellow.*

BATTLE HONOURS

VIMIERA	MARNE 1914
DOURO	AISNE 1914
TALAVERA	MESSINES 1914
FUENTES D'ONOR	YPRES 1914, 1915
SALAMANCA	CAMBRAI 1917, 1918
VITTORIA	
PYRENEES	SOMME 1918
ORTHES	AMIENS
PENINSULA	SAMBRE
CHILLIANWALLAH	TIGRIS 1916
GOOJERAT	KUT AL AMARA 1917
PUNJAB	
PERSIA	BAGHDAD
CENTRAL INDIA	MESOPOTAMIA 1915-18
SUAKIN 1885	PERSIA 1918
RELIEF OF LADYSMITH	BOLOGNA
SOUTH AFRICA 1900-02	MEDECINA
	ITALY 1945
MONS	
RETREAT OF MONS	

Distinctions

In 1799 the 14th Dragoons (forerunners of the 14th King's Hussars) were given the distinction of being allowed to wear the 'Prussian eagle' by Princess Frederica of Prussia, wife of the Duke of York. This distinction is still carried on today.

There are 35 battle honours emblazoned on the regimental drums, the latest engagement of the regiment being the Gulf War (1991) where they saw action against Iraqi forces with the band in support as medics.

Bandsman

The busby has a yellow fly with yellow piping, and a white plume.

The tunic has a dark blue collar and cuffs and a black pouch with a white metal 'Prussian eagle' in the centre. All chevrons are gold on scarlet backing.

The cavalry trousers are dark blue with two ¾" yellow stripes down each outer seam.

Bandmaster

The uniform of the Bandmaster is the same as that for the bandsman with the following differences.

All piping, frogging, loops and cap lines are gold. The epaulettes are of gold interwoven cord. The pouch belt and sword slings are gold regimental lace backed with yellow leather. The prickers and chain are silver, with all remaining fittings of white metal. The black pouch has a silver top with a gilt cypher in the centre. No badges of rank are worn.

The dark blue cavlary trousers have ¾" gold stripes down each outer seam.

Above: *The spectacular white plume of the Bandmaster.*

Left: *Front view of the Bandmaster in full ceremonial uniform.*

Right: *Rear view of the Bandmaster.*

Opposite page: *Fanfare trumpeter. The black Prussian Eagle is on a yellow background.*

15th/19th THE KING'S ROYAL HUSSARS

Colonel-in-Chief
HRH The Princess Margaret, Countess of Snowdon CI, DCVO

Motto
Merebimur (We shall be worthy)

History
Formed in April 1922 as the 15th/19th Hussars upon the amalgamation of the 15th the King's Hussars and the 19th (Queen Alexandra's Own Royal) Hussars. Re-designated the 15th King's Royal Hussars in October 1932 and finally designated the 15th/19th The King's Royal Hussars in December 1933.

Regimental Headquarters
Fenham Barracks, Newcastle-Upon-Tyne, Tyne & Wear NE2 4NP

Regimental Association
Fenham Barracks, Newcastle-Upon-Tyne, Tyne & Wear NE2 4NP

Regimental Museums
Fenham Barracks, Newcastle-Upon-Tyne, Tyne & Wear NE2 4NP
John George Joicey Museum, City Road, Newcastle-Upon-Tyne, Tyne & Wear

Marches
Quick march   'The Bold King's Hussars'
Slow march   'Eliott's Light Horse'
                'Denmark'

BATTLE HONOURS

EMSDORFF	MARNE 1914
MYSORE	AISNE 1914
VILLERS-EN-CAUCHIES	ARMENTIÈRES 1914
	YPRES 1914, 1915
WILLEMS	BELLEWAARDE
EGMONT OF ZEE	SOMME 1916, 1918
SERINGAPATAM	CAMBRAI 1917, 1918
SAHAGUN	ROSIÈRES
VITTORIA	AMIENS
NIAGARA	PURSUIT TO MONS
PENINSULA	FRANCE AND FLANDERS 1914-18
WATERLOO	
AFGHANISTAN 1878-80	WITHDRAWAL TO ESCAUT
EGYPT 1882, 1884	NEDERRIJN
ABU KLEA	RHINELAND
NILE 1884-5	HOCHWALD
DEFENCE OF LADYSMITH	RHINE
	IBBENBUREN
SOUTH AFRICA 1899-1902	ALLER
LE CATEAU	NORTH-WEST EUROPE 1940, 1944-5
RETREAT FROM MONS	

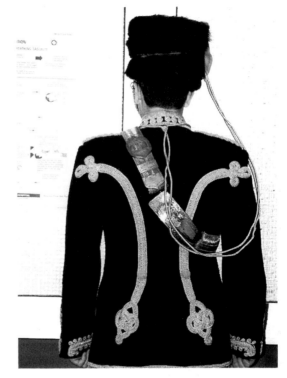

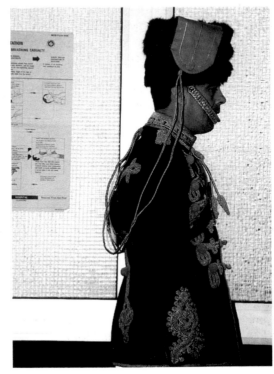

Top left: *Front view of the ceremonial uniform of the Bandmaster. Note the rich gold embroidery on the tunic and the absence of the scarlet plume.*
15th/19th KRH

Top right: *Rear view of Bandmaster.* 15th/19th KRH

Above: *Fanfare trumpet banner. Gold cyphers on blue garter on scarlet backing, the whole on dark blue cloth with gold fringe.* 15th/19th KRH

Right: *Side view of the Bandmaster.* 15th/19th KRH

Distinctions

The earliest record of the regimental band is in 1820, when the 14th King's Hussars formed a band and the Duke of Cumberland (then Colonel-In-Chief of the regiment) presented the first set of instruments. In actual fact the Duke had said 'Only German's alone can play the trumpet as it ought to be played, therefore it is impossible to form a band!' Needless to say the regiment proved him wrong.

There are 40 battle honours displayed upon the regimental drums.

Bandsman

The busby has a scarlet fly with yellow piping and a scarlet plume.

The tunic has a dark blue collar and cuffs. The pouch is white with a central cypher on scarlet backing. All chevrons are gold on a scarlet backing.

The cavalry trousers are dark blue with two ¾" yellow stripes down each outer seam.

Bandmaster

The uniform of the Bandmaster is the same as that for the bandsman with the following differences.

All piping, frogging, loops and cap lines are

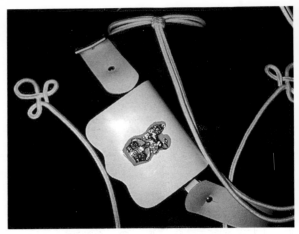

Top: *Detail of the O/R's pouch.*   15th/19th KHR
Below: *Side Drummer* and right, *Bass Drummer.*
15th/19th KRH
Opposite page: *The bass drum of the 15th/19th King's Royal Hussars, showing all panels.*
15th/19th KRH

gold. The collar and cuffs show heavy gold embroidery, such as that normally reserved for officer's tunics. The pouch belt and sword slings are of gold regimental lace backed with crimson leather. The prickers and chain are silver with all remaining fittings of white metal. The pouch is white leather with a silver top and gilt cypher in the centre. The epaulettes are of gold interwoven cord and no badges of rank are worn.

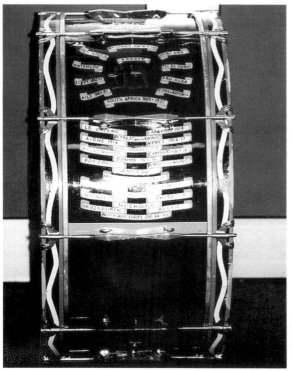

FORTHCOMING AMALGAMATIONS

On 4 July 1991 Tom King, the Defence Secretary, announced a dramatic change in the structure of the British Armed Forces. The changes primarily marked the amalgamation of many regiments, thus cutting the number of personnel. The cavalry regiments will be affected by the following amalgamations over the next two years.

The 4th/7th Royal Dragoon Guards and
      The 5th Royal Inniskilling Dragoon Guards
The 16th/5th The Queen's Royal Lancers and
      The 17th/21st Lancers
The Queen's Own Hussars and
      The Queen's Royal Irish Hussars
The Royal Hussars (Prince of Wales's Own) and
      The 14th/20th King's Hussars
The 13th/18th Royal Hussars (Queen Mary's Own) and
      The 15th/19th King's Royal Hussars

This final selection of photographs provides us with a last wistful look at what will soon be a bygone era.

Right: *Bandmasters in full ceremonial uniform at the Royal Tournament, 1991.* From left to right: *The Queen's Own Hussars, 4th/7th Royal Dragoon Guards and the 1st The Queen's Dragoon Guards.*

Below: *4th/7th Dragoon Guards, in Germany.*

13th/18th Royal Hussars (QMO) on parade.
13th/18th Royal Hussars (QMO)

Fanfare Trumpeters of the 17th/21st Lancers, rehearse the final fanfare at Knightsbridge Barracks, prior to the Cavalry Parade, 1992.